CONTENTS

Any words appearing in the text in bold, **like this**, are explained in the Glossary.

COMMUNICATIONS

Communications are ways of sending and receiving information. Important ones include television, radio, telephone (and **fax**), the **Internet** (and **e-mail**), post and newspapers.

This book is about radio. It examines how the radio programmes that people listen to are made and **broadcast**, the technology used and the people involved. It also looks at how radio is used in other forms of communications, such as television and telephones.

What is radio?

In the world of communications, radio means two things. First, it means the use of invisible **radio waves** to communicate between two places that may be very close together or thousands of kilometres apart. For example, radio waves carry communication between the crew of an ambulance and their headquarters. Second, it means radio broadcasting – which is how radio programmes are sent between radio stations and radios in homes and cars, normally using radio waves. When we listen to a radio, we are listening to sounds that are sent out from radio stations using broadcasting. Anybody with a radio **receiver** can listen to the sounds.

A small **studio** at a radio broadcasting station. It is organized so that everything the presenter needs during the show is in reach and ready to be used.

Communicating Today

Radio

Chris Oxlade

Heinemann
LIBRARY

www.heinemann.co.uk/library
Visit our website to find out more information about **Heinemann Library** books.

To order:
☎ Phone ++44 (0)1865 888066
▤ Send a fax to ++44 (0)1865 314091
▢ Visit the Heinemann Bookshop at www.heinemann.co.uk/library to browse our catalogue and order online.

First published in Great Britain by Heinemann Library, Halley Court, Jordan Hill, Oxford OX2 8EJ, a division of Reed Educational and Professional Publishing Ltd. Heinemann is a registered trademark of Reed Educational & Professional Publishing Ltd.

OXFORD MELBOURNE AUCKLAND JOHANNESBURG BLANTYRE
GABORONE IBADAN PORTSMOUTH NH (USA) CHICAGO

© Reed Educational and Professional Publishing Ltd 2001
The moral right of the proprietor has been asserted.

Designed by Visual Image
Illustrations by Visual Image
Originated by Ambassador Litho Ltd.
Printed in Hong Kong/China

06 05 04 03 02   06 05 04 03 02
10 9 8 7 6 5 4 3 2 1   10 9 8 7 6 5 4 3 2 1

ISBN 0431 11371 8 (hardback)   ISBN 0431 11378 5 (paperback)

British Library Cataloguing in Publication Data

Oxlade, Chris
  Radio. – (Communicating today)
  1. Radio – Juvenile literature
  I. Title
  621.3'84

Acknowledgements
The Publishers would like to thank the following for permission to reproduce photographs:
Corbis: pp4, 5, 9, 23, 28, James Marshall pp19, 25, Carl Purcell p24, Lynda Richardson p27, Bob Rowan p22; Hulton Getty: p29; Mike Kwasniak: p11; Peter Gould: p21; Photodisc: p18; PictureQuest/Stock Boston/Bohdan Hrynewych: p7; R.D. Battersby: p20; Sheena Verdun-Taylor: pp8, 12, 15; The Stock Market: p16; Stone: p26, Robert E Daemmrich p10, Don Smetzer p6; Telegraph Picture Library: p17.

Cover photograph reproduced with permission of Stone.

Every effort has been made to contact copyright holders of any material reproduced in this book. Any omissions will be rectified in subsequent printings if notice is given to the Publisher.

Emergency services such as the police and ambulance service make wide use of radio communications. This emergency worker is calling for assistance with a walkie-talkie radio.

Radio broadcasting brings us a wide range of entertainment and information programmes, such as dramas, sports coverage and game shows, news programmes, documentaries and education programmes. This book tells you how some typical radio programmes (a news **round-up**, a phone-in and a music show) are made, presented, **transmitted** and listened to. It also looks at how one of the stories in a news round-up, such as a story about the discovery of a hoard of old coins, is covered and reported.

After explaining radio broadcasting, the book looks at other radio communications, such as one-to-one radio used by emergency services. It also covers the science of radio waves, and how they are used in **telecommunications networks**.

RADIO BROADCASTING

All radio programmes, from **live** music shows to news documentaries, are made up of collections of sounds. These include live speech, recorded speech, music, sound effects, **jingles** and so on. Radio broadcasting is the process of making programmes with sound, and **transmitting** them so that people with radios can listen to them. It provides us with entertainment, news, information and education – 24 hours a day, almost wherever we are.

There are thousands of radio stations around the world. Many specialize in certain types of programme, such as music or news. Others offer a mixture of programmes. Some stations **broadcast** internationally, some nationally and some locally. National stations are often broadcast from several different local radio studios.

Some radio stations, such as those run by the BBC in the UK, are paid for by public money, but most are commercial. Commercial stations are funded by companies who pay to advertise their products, and by **sponsors**.

Anyone with a radio receiver can listen to programmes broadcast by radio. People listen to radio programmes at home on hi-fi sets such as this, on car radios, and while out and about on portable radios.

Sounds to the listener

The first stage in making a radio programme is to decide on the programme's contents and collect together the elements needed. For example, a news **round-up** programme needs elements such as news scripts for the newsreader, recorded interviews, and weather and travel reports. A music programme may just need CDs and a competition. A commercial station also needs advertisements ready to broadcast. During a radio programme, presenters or **producers** use such elements one after the other.

Radio programmes are sent to listeners using **radio waves**. A radio **receiver** detects the waves and turns them back into the original sounds, which people can listen to and enjoy. Some radio stations broadcast by television **satellite** and **cable**. Several thousand also broadcast through the **Internet**, which means they can be listened to anywhere in the world.

This disc-jockey, or DJ for short, is presenting a music programme. She talks into the microphone and plays different music tracks on the machines beside her.

GATHERING THE NEWS

A typical radio station **broadcasts** a half-hour news **round-up** programme in the early evening. It is also likely to broadcast a short news bulletin every hour throughout the day. Gathering news stories and reports is the job of the journalists who work in the radio station's newsroom.

In the newsroom

At a national radio station, there may be dozens of journalists working in the newsroom, including reporters, news **editors** (one each for general news, sport and so on) and newsreaders. At a local radio station, one person might do all these jobs.

New stories arrive in the newsroom all the time. They may come from the station's own reporters, **freelance** reporters, **press releases** and sometimes even from the station's listeners. They also come from news agencies – organizations that gather news stories and sell them to radio and television stations and newspapers. Radio newsrooms have an electronic link to the large news agencies. New stories from the agencies appear automatically on a printer or a computer screen.

This is the newsroom at a small radio station. The reporters and editors edit stories and present news programmes from here.

News reporters

An editor or team of editors decides what news stories should be included in the news round-up or bulletin, and also to which events to send reporters. Reporters collect information about a story, record interviews and write **copy** for the newsreader to read.

For example, news of the discovery of a hoard of old coins might arrive in the middle of the day. A reporter drives to the scene to cover the story. He or she finds out facts, such as who found the coins, how they were found, how many coins there were and how old they are. The reporter writes down these facts in a notebook and records an interview with the person who found the coins. Meanwhile, back in the newsroom, another reporter or editor might arrange for historians to be interviewed about other old coins found in the area.

The outside broadcast van of a small radio station. Inside, a reporter is interviewing a guest. The sounds can be recorded, sent live to the radio station for broadcast, or played to a crowd via **loudspeakers**.

RECORDING AND EDITING SOUNDS

News programmes (and many other radio programmes) are a mixture of **live** sounds, such as the presenter reading news headlines, and sounds that have been recorded earlier, such as interviews with people in the news. Recorded sounds are important for giving news programmes variety and interest.

Microphones

The first stage in recording a sound is to turn the pattern of vibrations that make up the sound into electricity. This is the job of a microphone. Inside the microphone a small metal plate vibrates as sound hits it. The vibrations are detected by an electronic circuit, which gives out a changing electric current called an **electrical signal**. The changes in the current represent the vibrations of the sound.

A reporter conducting an interview for radio with a portable cassette recorder. She is holding a microphone close to the speaker in order to pick up sound clearly.

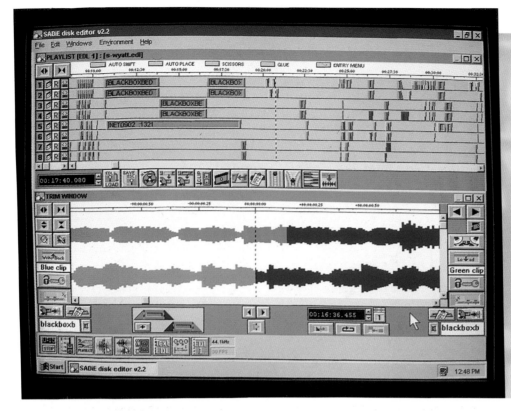

A screenshot from a computer program used to edit digital sounds. Sounds can be cut and pasted much like words can on a word processor.

Record and play back

To record a sound, the electrical signal is turned into a form that can be stored. For example, in a tape recorder, the signal is sent to an **electromagnet**. This creates a magnetic pattern in the magnetic coating on the tape as the tape moves past. In this way the sound is stored and can be played back.

Older recording equipment records electrical signals in analogue form, which means that the strength of the signal varies a great deal. In modern radio **studios**, sounds are stored in **digital** form, which uses a combination of the digits 0 and 1. Digital signals can be copied again and again without losing quality, and can also be stored in computer memory or on disk. They are easily **edited** on computer (see below).

Dubbing and editing

Reporters record reports and interviews on magnetic tape or digital sound recorders. When they return to the newsroom, they transfer them to tape or computer, which is called dubbing. Now the sound can be edited so that it lasts the correct amount of time for the news **round-up** or bulletin. The edited sound is stored ready for use.

IN A NEWS STUDIO

Radio news presenters work in a **studio** that is permanently set up for making news programmes. At a large or national radio station there is a **control room** next to the news studio, separated from it by a glass wall. The presenter sits in the studio and a news **producer** sits in the control room. The presenter reads the news and conducts interviews while the producer operates the technical equipment. At a local radio station which presents only short news bulletins, one person may both present the news and operate the technical equipment.

Studio equipment

A news studio contains several microphones so that several presenters, reporters and expert guests can take part in discussions. Microphones are very sensitive to sound, so the people in the studio must be careful not to knock over chairs, rustle their clothes or slam the studio door. They wear earphones so that they can hear what is being **broadcast** as well as instructions to them from the producer.

This is a mixing desk in a radio studio. In the centre are sliding controls that adjust the volume of the sound from different sources, such as microphones and telephone lines.

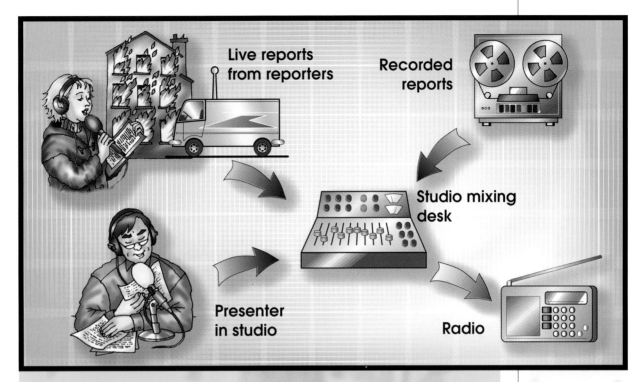

Live reports from reporters

Recorded reports

Studio mixing desk

Presenter in studio

Radio

The sounds that you hear on your radio come from many different sources. They all go to a mixing desk, where the presenter or producer controls which ones you hear.

A modern studio also contains computer screens where the presenter can see **copy** for news stories, the running order of the programme and other useful information, such as **e-mails** from listeners.

Studio controls

Each microphone in the studio is connected to a **mixing desk**. Here, the presenter or producer uses sliding controls to 'open' a microphone so that signals from it are broadcast, or 'close' it so that they are not broadcast. Also connected to the mixing desk are communication lines to other studios and a telephone switchboard.

Audio clips – short pieces of sound that have already been recorded, such as interviews, **jingles** and advertisements – are stored on computer or on short loops of recording tape inside tape cartridges. The presenter or producer plays the clips stored on computer by touching the relevant picture on a touch-sensitive screen, and plays the clips stored on tape cartridges by pressing them into a cartridge machine.

BROADCASTING THE NEWS

Once the news is gathered, the reports are recorded, the **copy** written, and the **studio** ready, a news **round-up** programme can be **broadcast**. The running order for a typical programme is shown below. It shows what time each segment of the programme starts, how long it lasts and who reads the copy.

For example, a story about finding a hoard of coins might begin exactly nine minutes into the programme. It includes a short introduction (called a cue) by the presenter, an introduction by the reporter, a short interview with the person who found the coins, and finishes with the reporter's summary. It is timed to last exactly two minutes. The presenter is told the last words of the report so that he or she knows exactly when the story finishes.

Time (mins : secs)	Programme section
00.00	Opening music
00.30	News summary (presenter)
03.30	Travel and weather (travel and weather person)
05.00	Recorded advertisements
07.00	Live news report (reporter)
09.00	Recorded news report
11.00	News interview (presenter)
13.00	Recorded advertisements
15.30	News summary (presenter)
18.30	Travel and weather (travel and weather person)
20.00	Sports news (sports reporter)
23.00	Recorded advertisements
25.00	Recorded news report
27.00	News interview (presenter)
29.00	Headlines (presenter)
29.30	Closing music
30.00	Programme ends

A newsreader presenting the news in a studio. He reads the script on the desk, and also works the mixing desk so that he can talk to guests and reporters.

Reading copy

The copy that the presenter reads is written very clearly so that it is easy to read from paper or a computer screen. For example, the figure 2,000,000 is written as 2 million to save the presenter trying to count the zeros. The presenter will try to rehearse reading the copy before reading it out **live** during the broadcast.

In control

In the **control room**, the **producer** makes sure that recordings such as reports, advertisements and **jingles** are ready to play (this is called cueing), and plays them when they are needed. He or she also opens and closes microphones and makes connections to reporters and interviewees on the telephone or in other studios.

PHONE-INS AND MUSIC

On these pages you can find out how a typical phone-in programme and a music programme are **broadcast**. These need different equipment from a news **round-up** programme and so are often broadcast from specialized **studios**.

At a typical radio station, the programmes are broadcast one after the other, with a five-minute news bulletin between them. The bulletin is presented from a separate studio by a newsreader, and includes a short recorded report from a reporter about the story that was covered in more detail in the news round-up. There are also advertisement breaks at regular intervals throughout both programmes.

People phone into radio stations to try to win prizes, talk to famous guests, ask for songs to be played, and express their opinions on talk shows.

Collecting calls

For a phone-in programme, a studio assistant has the job of answering telephone calls from listeners who want to take part. The assistant notes down the caller's name, where they are from, and brief details of what points they want to make on air. This information is entered into a computer and appears on a screen in the studio. The presenter selects callers from the screen by touching the screen or by using a **mixing desk**. The phone system allows several callers to be **live** on air at the same time.

Phone-ins are often broadcast with a delay of several seconds between the studio and the **transmitter**. This allows transmission to be stopped if a caller says anything that the presenter feels may be offensive to other listeners.

A presenter using a mixing desk. He is operating a sliding control that adjusts the volume of his voice or the music he is playing.

Playing music

Music programmes are presented from a studio equipped with CD-players and turntables for vinyl records. Before presenting the programme, a list of songs to be played has to be written up, with timings for each one, so that the programme will last for the correct time. During transmission the presenter has to fade the tracks up and down using the mixing desk. One of the skills they need is to be able to talk between the tracks without talking over the lyrics (song-words) at the end of one song or at the beginning of the next.

17

WAVES AND BANDS

Radio broadcasting and other forms of communications use **radio waves** to send sounds and other information from place to place. Radio waves are invisible waves that travel at the speed of light (300,000 kilometres per second), and can pass through solid objects.

There is a whole range of different radio waves, all with different wavelengths. Wavelength is the distance between the crest of one wave and the crest of the next, measured in metres. For communications, these waves are divided into groups, called wavebands, named after the type of wave in them, such as short wave, long wave, and very high **frequency** (VHF) wave. Different types of radio communications use waves in different bands.

Radio signals are sent out from a transmitter. Transmitters are placed on the top of tall towers so that the signals can spread out without hills or buildings getting in the way.

These model ships are controlled by radio waves. The wavelengths of the radio waves used for them are different from those used for radio broadcasting.

Transmitting signals

Radio waves are the link between a radio station and the radios of people who listen to it. At the radio station **studio**, **electrical signals** from different sources (microphones, CD-players and so on) are mixed to create a signal that will be **broadcast** to the listeners. This signal is sent to the station's **transmitter**, which sends out the radio waves.

Modulation

The radio waves from a transmitter are like a vehicle that carries the signal from the studio to radio **receivers**. In fact, they are called carrier waves. To make a carrier wave carry the signal, it is shaped to match the signal. This shaping process is called modulation.

A carrier wave is made by an electronic circuit called an oscillator. This wave is modulated (shaped) by the electrical signal from the studio. Then it is **amplified** by more electronic circuits, and sent to the transmitter's **aerial**. The strong electrical signal creates a radio signal that spreads out from the aerial.

RECEIVING SIGNALS

A radio **receiver** detects **radio waves** coming from a radio station and turns them back into the sounds that were originally made in the radio station's **studio**.

Aerials

All radio receivers need an **aerial**. To receive stations **broadcast** in **FM**, they need a long wire aerial. To receive stations broadcast in **AM**, they need a different aerial that is normally inside the radio's case. When radio signals hit the aerial, they create tiny **electrical signals** inside it. These signals are the same as the shaped carrier signals that were made at the **transmitter**, but millions of times weaker because they have spread out so much.

Tuning

To listen to a radio station, you need to know its **frequency** so that you can select the station on your radio receiver (which is

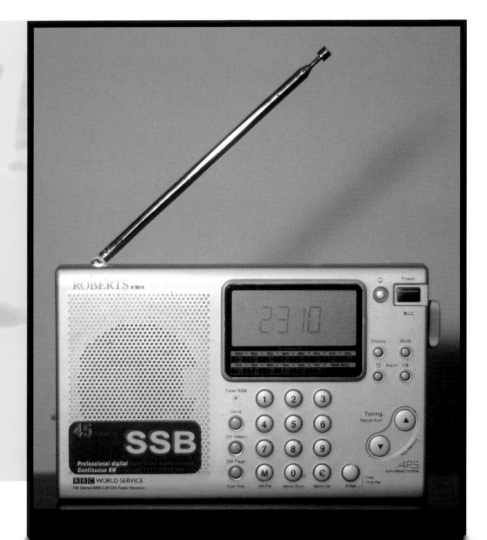

The aerial on top of this radio is for detecting FM signals. It needs to be extended to pick up weak signals properly.

called tuning). The frequencies are shown on the radio's dial or display, in kilohertz (kHz) or megahertz (MHz).

Tuning means selecting signals from the radio station that you want to listen to. When you turn a radio's tuning dial or press its tuning buttons, you are adjusting an electronic circuit called a tuning circuit, making it collect signals of a certain frequency and ignore all the others. Once the radio has collected the correct carrier signal, it gets the original signal that represents the sound from its carrier signal. This is called demodulation, and is the opposite of modulation. The signal is then **amplified** and sent to a **loudspeaker**, where it is turned back into sound.

So, finally, the listener hears the sound made in the radio studio, just a fraction of a second after it was made.

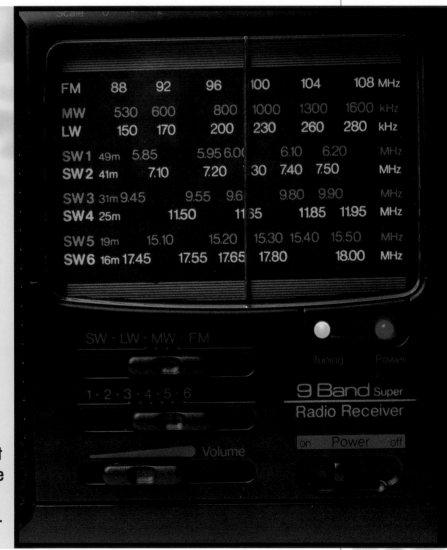

This radio can receive programmes broadcast on many different bands. Short wave (SW) bands are used to broadcast international stations.

ONE-TO-ONE RADIO

Broadcast radio is a one-way type of communications system. Signals travel from radio stations to their listeners, but the listeners cannot send sounds back to the radio station. With one-to-one radio systems, however, people can have conversations by radio, because the radio sets used can both send and receive signals.

Walkie-talkie radio

The simplest one-to-one radio system is walkie-talkie radio. The hand-held walkie-talkie sets send radio signals in much the same way that radio stations broadcast sound. The person's voice is turned into a signal that is carried by **radio waves**. The waves spread in all directions and are detected by the **aerial** of the other set, wherever it is. Both sets need a **transmitter** and a **receiver**, and must be tuned so that the **frequency** of the carrier waves sent by each set is the same as the frequency that they are set to receive.

The main disadvantage of walkie-talkie radios is that they are powered by small batteries and so **transmit** only weak signals. This means that they work only over a range of a few kilometres.

A simple walkie-talkie set contains a microphone, a small loudspeaker, a tuning dial and an aerial on top. The user presses a button when he wants to speak and releases it to listen.

Thousands of Australian families live in their country's outback, a long way from any town. Many children have lessons at home and talk to their teachers by radio.

Radio networks

When a radio **network** is set up, a radio operator at a central control room can communicate with any member of the service who is carrying a walkie-talkie radio set. Radio sets in vehicles work over a longer range than walkie-talkie radios because they work from the vehicles' electrical system.

One-to-one radio has many different uses, but it is perhaps most important for members of the emergency services, such as ambulance drivers and fire-fighters, who use it to keep in contact with each other. Mobile telephones would be unsuitable for these jobs because they cannot be used in remote areas and would become useless if the telephone network developed a fault. One-to-one radio is also used by air-traffic controllers to talk to pilots. Each control centre uses a different frequency so that the pilot can tune to different centres as the plane flies along its route.

RADIO IN COMMUNICATIONS

Radio waves are also used in types of communications other than radio **broadcasting** and one-to-one radio. These include television, where radio waves carry pictures from television stations to television **receivers**, and the telephone, where radio waves form many of the links in the **telecommunications network**.

Radio in the telecommunications network

The telecommunications network is the network that carries telephone calls, **e-mails**, **fax** messages and computer **data** around the world. Telephones and telephone exchanges are connected together by communications channels, in the form of electrical cables, optical-fibre cables and radio waves.

These huge dishes are at a satellite television station. They send signals tens of thousands of kilometres into space. The signals are sent as microwaves that are focused into a beam by the dish.

Most radio links in the telecommunications network use radio waves of high **frequency**, called microwaves. Microwaves are effective because they can be focused into narrow beams and aimed to travel from a **transmitter** to a receiver. Microwave links between telephone exchanges have a transmitter and receiver at each end. The dish-shaped **aerials** for the transmitters and receivers are mounted on tall buildings or hill-top masts so that there is a direct line of sight between the transmitters and receivers.

Microwaves are also used to carry signals up to telecommunications **satellites** from ground stations, and from the satellites back to the ground.

Radio for mobiles

A mobile telephone hand-set is a combination of a telephone and a walkie-talkie radio. Sounds (and often data, too) travel to and from the hand-set to the closest fixed aerial of the mobile-phone network as radio waves. The landscape is divided into areas called cells, each with its own aerial. This is why mobile telephones are often called cell phones. These fixed aerials are linked into the normal telephone network.

Pagers also work with radio waves, which are **transmitted** from a central control system. Each pager operated by a paging company has an identity code. It receives radio waves with an in-built aerial. If it detects a signal containing its own code, it sounds an alarm, and displays a message sent from central control.

This is a microwave relay tower that is part of a telephone network. The dishes collect microwaves from distant relay towers, make them stronger and send them off to other relay towers.

INFORMATION BY RADIO

Radio waves are used not only for communicating sounds and pictures between people and computers, but also for controlling machines and sending information between machines. Examples of this include radio control, telemetry and navigation systems.

Radio control

To make a model plane, car or boat move, the user moves switches and dials on a hand-set which sends specific radio signals out from the set's **transmitter**. A **receiver** in the model detects the signals and activates the motors that move the model's parts.

Remote control is also useful for sending machines into places that are too dangerous or difficult for humans to explore. For example, smoke-filled buildings or shipwrecks in the depths of the sea can be explored by remote-controlled machines that carry cameras.

Unmanned spacecraft, such as the probes that land on other planets, are also controlled by radio, though the signals may take many minutes to arrive because of the huge distances involved. These spacecraft often send pictures back to the controlling station by radio.

An air-traffic control system uses radio waves to detect the position and speed of aircraft. The aircraft send radio signals to tell the system which aeroplane is which.

A radio transmitter attached to the shell of a turtle. The transmitter will send out a signal that will allow researchers to track the turtle's movements.

Telemetry

Telemetry is the process of sending readings by radio from scientific instruments to distant places where the readings can be read or recorded. For example, **data** can be sent back to the ground from weather-measuring instruments (such as thermometers and barometers) carried by a weather balloon high up in the atmosphere. Data from the instruments is turned into **electrical signals** and **transmitted** as radio waves, just as sound is transmitted from a radio station.

Navigation

Radio is useful for navigating and for tracking objects. For example, the **satellites** of the Global Positioning System (GPS) send radio signals down to the Earth's surface. A GPS receiver detects the different signals from various satellites and uses the signals to work out its position very accurately. Aircraft also use radio navigation systems to work out their position and to guide their pilots safely down to runways in bad weather.

Radio tracking systems use receivers to detect signals coming from radio transmitters that have been attached to moving objects. Applications of tracking systems include tracking stolen cars and tracking animals to research their movements.

RADIO TIMES

Here are some of the major events and technical developments in the history of radio.

1864 British physicist James Clerk Maxwell predicts that **radio waves** exist, although he does not prove it. He also claims they are related to light and travel at the speed of light, which we now know is true.

1888 German physicist Heinrich Hertz proves that radio waves exist.

1896 Italian scientist Guglielmo Marconi is the first person to demonstrate that radio waves can be used for communication. He sends a simple Morse code message between two **aerials** several kilometres apart.

1901 Marconi sends a Morse code message (consisting of the letter 's') from Britain to Canada by radio. The radio waves are sent between two 60-metre high aerials, one in each country.

Guglielmo Marconi needed very long wire aerials for his early experiments. He devised a way of raising one end of an aerial into the air using large kites.

1906 Reginald Fessenden, from Canada, develops the idea of modulation (which enables radio waves to communicate sounds) and makes the first-ever radio **broadcast**.

early 1920s A few people have simple radio **receivers** and are listening to broadcasts from the first regular radio stations.

1922 The British Broadcasting Corporation (BBC) starts its radio broadcasts in the UK.

1950s The first small and cheap transistor-based radios (nicknamed 'trannies') are made, enabling people to carry a radio anywhere with them.

1962 Television pictures are relayed across the Atlantic using radio signals by the Telstar communications **satellite**.

1997 Radio stations begin **transmitting** over the **Internet** as well as by radio waves.

A transistor radio from the 1950s. The radio is huge compared to a modern portable radio, but it was smaller and lighter than any radios before it.

GLOSSARY

aerial length of wire, metal rod or coil of wire, that creates or detects radio waves

AM short for amplitude modulation, a way of making a radio wave carrying a signal by varying its amplitude (strength)

amplify make larger or more powerful

broadcast 1) to transmit signals that people with radio receivers can detect. 2) A programme that is transmitted.

cable way of broadcasting by sending signals along cables

control room room separated from a studio by a glass wall. It contains the equipment needed to broadcast a radio programme

copy the words that a presenter reads

data facts or information

digital 1) signal that is made up of on and off pulses of electricity, represented by the binary digits 0 and 1. 2) Any information stored in the form of the binary digits 0 and 1.

e-mail short for electronic mail, a system that allows people to send written messages to each other's computers via the Internet

edit to cut or move around pieces of sound until they last for a required length of time

editor person who decides what stories to include in the news programme and edits words or sounds

electrical signal changing electric current that represents a sound

electromagnet magnet made of coils of wire. It can be turned on and off by turning on and off the electricity flowing round the coil.

fax short for facsimile, a system that allows pages of text and pictures to be sent along a telephone line

FM short for frequency modulation, a way of making a radio wave carry a signal by varying its frequency

freelance not employed by one company or organization, but working for several

frequency number of cycles of a wave per second

Internet global computer network that allows people with computers linked to it to access information on any other computer around the world

jingle short piece of music or song lasting a few seconds that is played before or during segments of radio programmes

live describes sounds of events that are broadcast to radio receivers as the events happen

loudspeaker device that turns an electrical signal that represents a sound back into sound

mixing desk machine with sliding buttons which controls what sounds radio listeners hear

network system of interconnected transmitters and receivers

press release information about an event or news story written and distributed by a person, company or organization

producer person who co-ordinates a radio programme and works the technical equipment, such as the mixing desk

radio waves invisible electromagnetic waves that can pass through the air and space

receiver 1) short for radio receiver, a device that detects radio waves and turns them back into sounds. 2) Any device that collects signals and turns them back into pictures or sounds.

round-up summary of all the latest news stories

satellite object that orbits around the Earth in space

sponsor person, company or organization that gives money to a radio station in return for their name being mentioned regularly on air, on the station's posters and so on

studio room in a radio station from which programmes are broadcast

telecommunications communication systems that use electricity or electronics to work, such as radio, television and the telephone

transmit to send out radio waves

transmitter machine that sends out radio waves

INDEX